A QUESTRON™ ELECTRONIC

MY FIRST BOOK OF SPELLING

PRICE/STERN/SLOAN
Publishers, Inc., Los Angeles

DISTRIBUTED BY
RANDOM HOUSE, INC.
New York

THE QUESTRON™ SYSTEM
COMBINING FUN WITH LEARNING

This book is part of **THE QUESTRON SYSTEM**, which offers children a unique aid to learning and endless hours of challenging entertainment.

The QUESTRON electronic "wand" uses a microchip to sense correct and incorrect answers with "right" or "wrong" sounds and lights. Victory sounds and lights reward the user when particular sets of questions or games are completed. Powered by a nine-volt alkaline battery, which is activated only when the wand is pressed on a page, QUESTRON should have an exceptionally long life. The QUESTRON ELECTRONIC WAND can be used with any book in the QUESTRON series.

A note to parents...

With QUESTRON, right or wrong answers are indicated instantly and can be tried over and over to reinforce learning and improve skills. Children need not be restricted to the books designated for their age group, as interests and rates of development vary widely. Also, within many of the books, certain pages are designed for the older end of the age group and will provide a stimulating challenge to younger children.

Many activities are designed at different levels. For example, the child can select an answer by recognizing a letter or by reading an entire word. The activities for pre-readers and early readers are intended to be used with parental assistance. Interaction with parents or older children will stimulate the learning experience.

QUESTRON Project Director: Roger Burrows
Editorial Coordinators/Art Directors: Lee A. Scott, Judy Walker
Writer: Lee A. Scott
Illustrator: Meredith Johnson
Educational Consultant: Beverley Dietz

Copyright ©1986 by Price/Stern/Sloan Publishers, Inc. All rights reserved under International and Pan-American Copyright Conventions. No part of this publication may be reproduced, stored in a retrieval system, or transmitted in any form or by any means, electronic, mechanical, photocopying, recording or otherwise, without the prior written permission of the publisher. Published by Price/Stern/Sloan Publishers, Inc., 410 North La Cienega Boulevard, Los Angeles, California 90048. Distributed by Random House, Inc., 201 East 50th Street, New York, New York 10022. ISBN: 0-394-88171-0
1 2 3 4 5 6 7 8 9 0

QUESTRON™ is a trademark of Price/Stern/Sloan Publishers, Inc.
U.S.A. and International Patents Pending
Manufactured in the U.S.A.

HOW TO START QUESTRON

Hold **QUESTRON** at this angle and press the activator button firmly on the page.

Battery Door (When QUESTRON begins to malfunction, add a new 9-volt alkaline battery. To open battery door, pull base up slightly and slide out.)

Speaker

Lights

Activator Button

Sensors (Keep clean with a soft brush.)

HOW TO USE QUESTRON

PRESS
Press **QUESTRON** firmly on the shape below, then lift it off.

TRACK
Press **QUESTRON** down on "Start" and keep it pressed down as you move to "Finish."

RIGHT & WRONG WITH QUESTRON

Press **QUESTRON** on the square.

See the green light and hear the sound. This green light and sound say "You are correct."

Press **QUESTRON** on the circle.

Hear the victory sound. Don't be dazzled by the flashing lights. You deserve them.

Press **QUESTRON** on the triangle.

The red light and sound say "Try again." Lift **QUESTRON** off the page and wait for the sound to stop.

Easy as ABC!

Look at the first letter of each word. Press **Questron** on the answer box with the words in the correct **abc** order.

Skill: Alphabetizing by first letter

DEFGHIPT
jklmnopqrstuvwxyz

What's Missing?

Look at each picture. Find the missing letter to complete the word that goes with each picture. Press **Questron** on the correct letter.

_ow

k c o

_ig

g b p

_ed

d b p

t_p

e o a

j_g

n r u

b_y

c o u

cu_

p d g

bo_

v w x

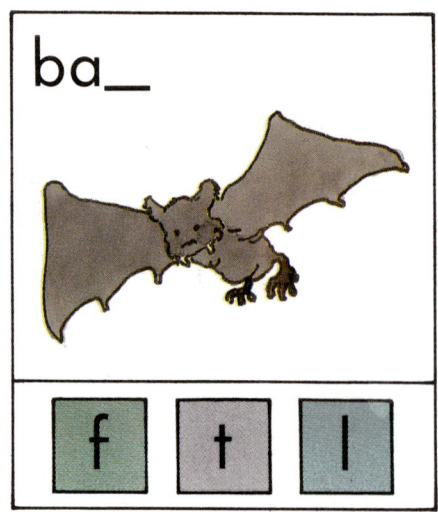
ba_

f t l

Skill: Recognizing and spelling object words

b_rd

| i | e | y |

f__rm

| a | i | o |

bab_

| i | e | y |

bo_t

| o | i | a |

f_og

| r | h | n |

t_o

| w | o | u |

g_rl

| u | i | e |

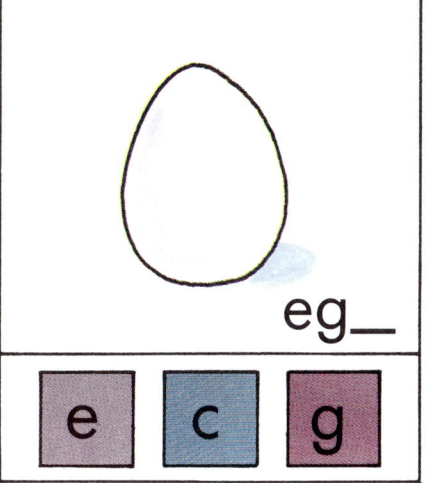

eg_

| e | c | g |

pon_

| i | y | e |

7

What's Different?

Look at each row of words. Press **Questron** on the word that is different.

big	big	big	dig	big
cap	cap	cab	cap	cap
dine	dine	dine	dine	pine
map	map	mad	map	map
jam	jaw	jam	jam	jam
sip	sip	zip	sip	sip
press	dress	dress	dress	dress
green	green	green	queen	green

Skill: Word recognition

Word Shapes

Look at the word at the beginning of each row. Press **Questron** on the shape in that row that matches the word.

| long |
| what |
| cold |
| feel |
| clock |
| apple |

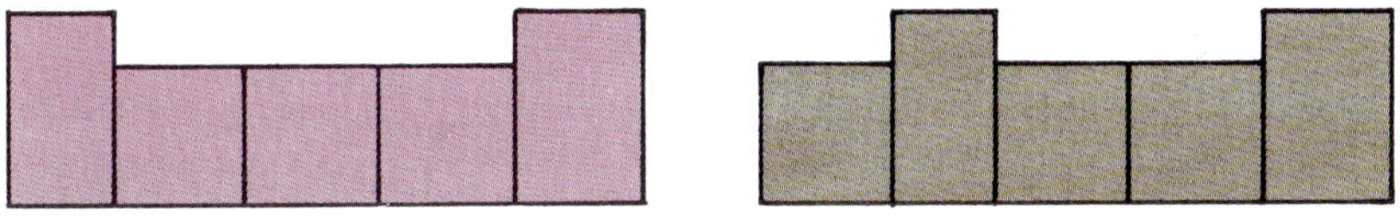

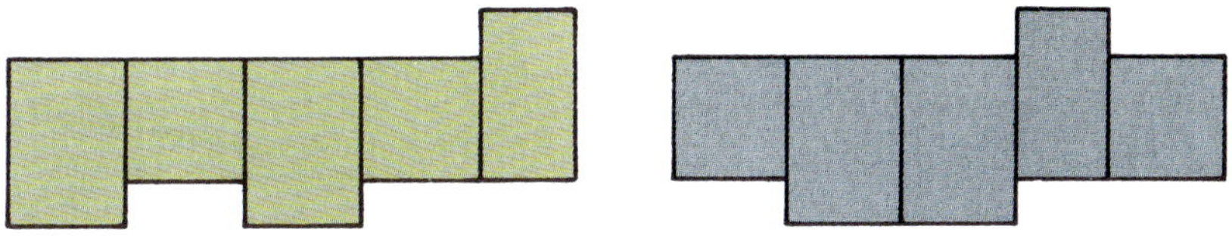

Skill: Recognizing whole word configurations

Word Wall

Look at each pair of words. Are the letters in the same order or are they different? Press **Questron** on pairs that are different.

bag gab	stop spot
on no	fast fast
here here	lost lots	now won
first first	much much
like like	there three
with with	not ton	best bets
very very	shoe hoes
bare bear	but tub	come come
nose nose	ram arm
good good

10

Skill: Visual sequencing

Word Match

Look at the word in the first box in each row. Press **Questron** on the word in that row that is the same.

who	how	who	ohw
has	ash	sah	has
own	own	now	won
was	saw	was	aws
eat	ate	eat	tea
stop	spot	tops	stop
came	meac	came	eamc
there	there	theer	three

Skill: Visual discrimination/letter sequencing.

Party Time!

Press **Questron** on the words that are spelled correctly.

Rosie gave a costume party. All her friends came dressed up. They played games. They ate ice cream and cake. Everyone had a good time.

Sally dressed up as an apple.

Sally dressed up as an appel.   apple.

Henry ate four pieces of cake.

Henry ate four   fuor pieces of cake.

Jake played with the blue monster.

Jake played wiht   with the blue   bleu monster.

Skill: Recognizing and spelling basic sight vocabulary

The bear hid behind the chair.

The [bear] [baer] hid behind the [chair.] [chiar.]

Bernie stood on his head.

Bernie stood [no] [on] his [head.] [haed.]

Barbara made noise with her horn.

Barbara made [niose] [noise] with her [horn.] [honr.]

The little magician did eight tricks.

The [little] [littel] magician did [eight] [eigth] tricks.

The first robot danced with the third robot.

The [frist] [first] robot danced with the [third] [thrid] robot.

1, 2, 3 Go!

The word on each door is spelled correctly. Press **Questron** on the wheel with the word that matches the correctly spelled word.

Skill: Visual discrimination/letter sequencing.

Signs of the City

Press **Questron** on the signs with the correctly spelled words.

Skill: Recognizing and spelling basic sight vocabulary

Missing Letters

There is one darker word in each sentence. Can you spell it? Press **Questron** on the missing letter to complete the word.

Sandy and Morton **walk** to the park.	w_lk a o	_alk v w	wa_k l t
They see a **sign**, "Balloons for Sale."	s_gn y i	si_n u g	sig_ r n
They **buy** four balloons.	b_y n u	bu_ i y	_uy d b
Morton **would** like to have the orange one.	wo_ld o u	wou_d l t	woul_ b d
Does Sandy have **three** balloons?	t_ree h k	_hree t f	thr_e i e
I think **their** balloons are pretty.	_heir f t	th_ir u e	the_r i e

Skill: Spelling basic sight vocabulary

Silent Search

Say each word. Which letters are silent? Help the detective. Press **Questron** on the silent letters.

talk
write
night
castle
light
comb
high
know
sign
stage
lamb
knight

Skill: Recognizing and identifying silent letters

On Your Mark...

How fast can you finish the course? Follow the path. Read each word. Press **Questron** on the correctly spelled words. If you make a mistake, start over.

Skill: Recognizing basic sight vocabulary

On the Ball

Which words are spelled correctly? Track **Questron** on those words in each maze. Start on the ★.

The first letter of each correctly spelled word spells a mystery word. Can you solve each mystery?

★	catch	ice	theer
	fram	rabbit	sopt
	deks	came	under
	raed	littel	show

★	peanut	fof	drest
	apple	tohn	every
	read	again	door
	fli	cak	brid

Skill: Recognizing and spelling basic sight vocabulary

Which One?

Look at each picture. Read each sentence. The letter in each answer box will make a word. Which word is the best choice to complete the sentence? Press **Questron** on the letter that completes the word.

John wore his __at out to play.

b   c   r   h

Tom is as __all as a tree.

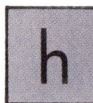 
h   t   f   b

Judy can __ake an apple pie.

c   l   b   w

The band will __ead the parade.

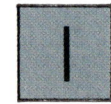   
l   r   m   b

Skill: Word discrimination

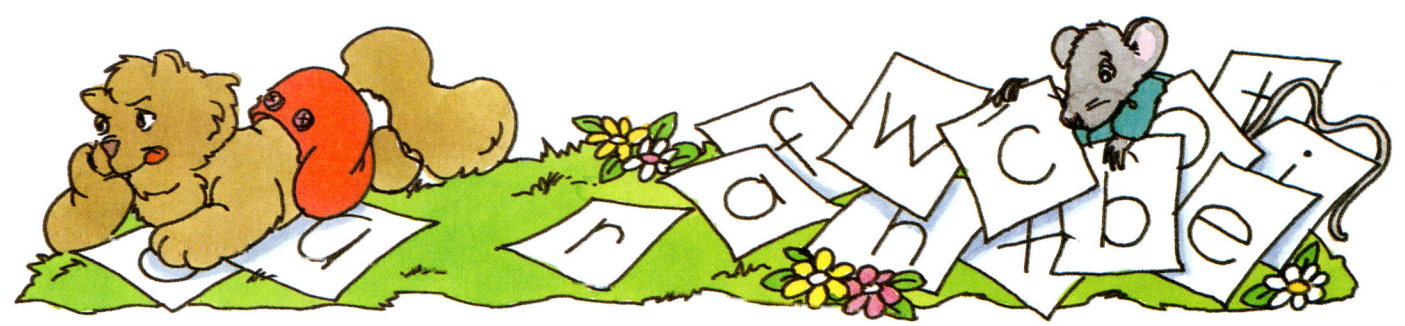

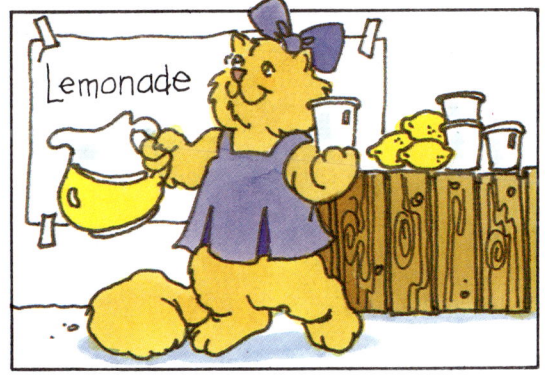

Lee _old the most lemonade.

c s h t

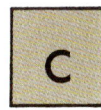

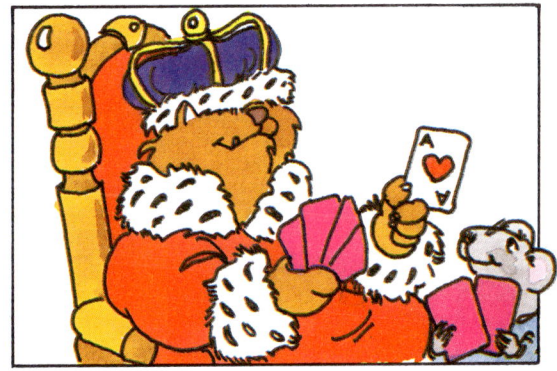

The _ing played Hearts.

k r w d

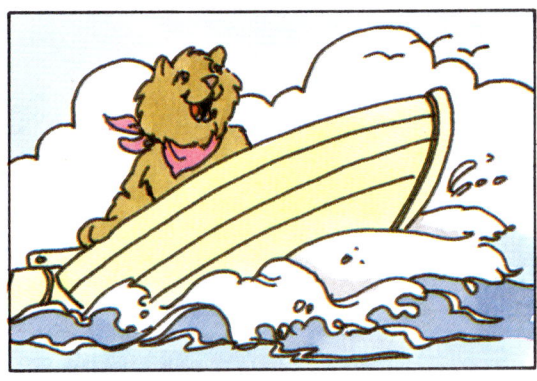

The boat floated in on the _ide.

t s w r

Roger is having a _ood time.

w g f h

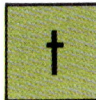

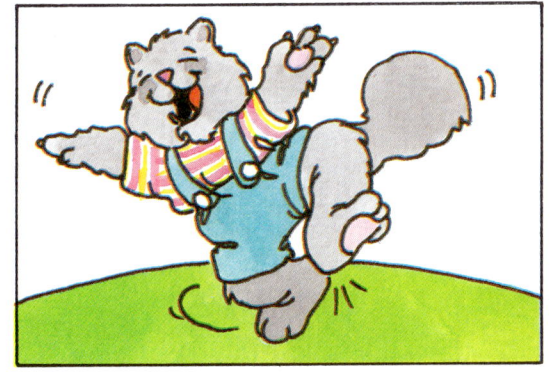

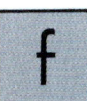

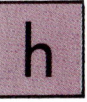

Spell It Right

Look at each picture. Press **Questron** on the answer box with the correctly spelled word.

asleep | aslepe

brokin | broken

bicycle | bycicle

block | blok

bread | braed

scate | skate

kitchin | kitchen

ladder | lader

leaves | leeves

Skill: Recognition and spelling of basic sight vocabulary

AT BATCAT

mowse | mouse

puppet | pupat

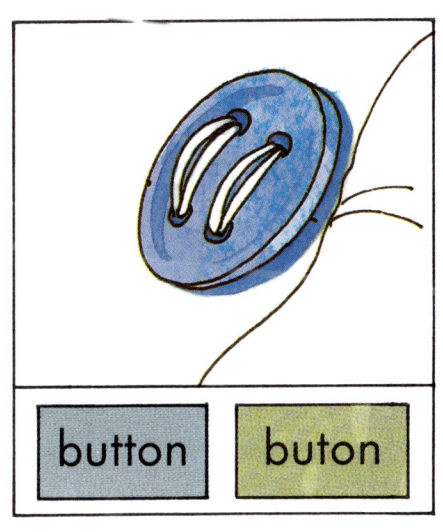

button | buton

clothes | clothez

monee | money

table | tabel

guce | goose

lion | lyon

pial | pail

Shop and Spell

Annie has made a list of things she wants to buy at the store. Press **Questron** on the words that are spelled correctly.

- eggs
- braed
- toothpaste
- lunch bags
- aminal cookies
- milk
- chiken
- string
- birthday candels
- flowers
- fluor
- buter

Skill: Recognizing and spelling basic sight vocabulary

Better Letter

Peter is on vacation. He wrote a letter to his friend. Can you help him find the 7 words he spelled incorrectly. Press **Questron** on the words that are spelled incorrectly, so Peter can fix them.

Dear John,

Aunt Penny let me fede the pigs and play with the gote. They have lots of cows and horses. I had to get up early in the morning to mikl the cows. Uncel Henry is going to let me ride on the tractor when he plows the field. I'm going to run and jump in the hay. Theer is an apple tree with a swing. Aunt Penny is a dood cook. I'm having a great time.

Your freind,

Peter

Skill: Visual discrimination/letter sequencing

Spelling Bee

Some words are even hard for grown-ups to spell. Can you guess what these long, hard-to-spell words mean? Press **Questron** on the answer you think is correct.

kindergarten

a class in school

a box to grow flowers

pretzel

a machine that makes pickles

a salted knot-shaped biscuit

dictionary

a book that shows how to spell words

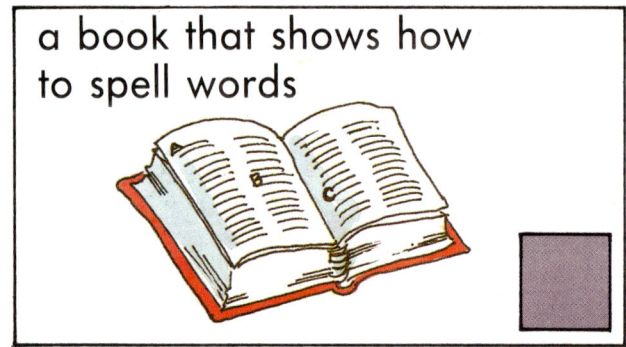

a funny animal

Skill: Recognizing and understanding difficult words

parallelogram

a type of radio	a special four-sided shape
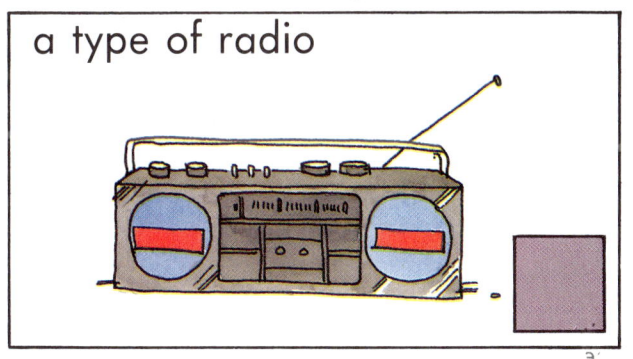	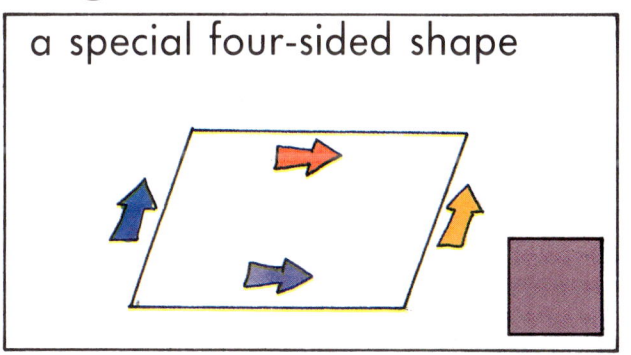

gallinaceous

like a turkey	a pop rock group

hippopotamus

a tall building with a pointed roof	a large animal with short legs

THE QUESTRON LIBRARY OF ELECTRONIC BOOKS

A series of books specially designed to
reach — and teach — and entertain children of all ages

QUESTRON ELECTRONIC WORKBOOKS

Early Childhood	Grades K-5
My First Counting Book	My First Reading Book (K-1)
My First ABC Book	My First Book of Telling Time (1-3)
My First Book of Animals	Day of the Dinosaur (K-3)
Shapes and Sizes	First Grade Skills (1)
Preschool Skills	My First Book of Addition (1-2)
My First Vocabulary	The Storytime Activity Book (1-3)
My First Nursery Rhymes	My Robot Book (1-3)
Autos, Ships, Trains and Planes	My First Book of Spelling (1-3)
Reading Readiness	My First Book of Subtraction (1-3)
My First Words	My First Book of Multiplication (2-3)
My First Numbers	I Want to Be... (2-5)
Going Places	Number Fun (2-5)
Kindergarten Skills	Word Fun (2-5)

ELECTRONIC QUIZBOOKS FOR THE WHOLE FAMILY

Trivia Fun and Games
How, Why, Where and When
More How, Why, Where and When
World Records and Amazing Facts

PRICE/STERN/SLOAN — **RANDOM HOUSE, INC.**
Publishers, Inc., Los Angeles   *New York*